Yellow Umbrella Books are published by Capstone Press
151 Good Counsel Drive, P.O. Box 669, Mankato, Minnesota 56002
http://www.capstone-press.com

1 2 3 4 5 6 07 06 05 04 03 02

Library of Congress Cataloging-in-Publication Data
Trumbauer, Lisa, 1963–
   Graph it!/by Lisa Trumbauer.
   p. cm. —(Math)
   Summary: Eas-to-read text and photographs present a picture graph, a pie graph, and a bar graph.
   Includes index.
   ISBN 0-7368-1282-2
   1. Graphic methods—Juvenile literature. [1. Graphic methods.] I. Title. II. Series.
QA90 .T78 2002
511′ .5—dc 21
                                               2001008284

Editorial Credits
Susan Evento, Managing Editor/Product Development; Elizabeth Jaffe, Senior Editor; Dawn Harris, Designer; Kimberly Danger and Heidi Schoof, Photo Researchers

Photo Credits
Cover: Cathy Gyory; Title Page: Tom McCarthy/Unicorn Stock (top left), Ernest A. Janes/Bruce Coleman (top right), Uniphoto (bottom left), Bill Beatty/Visuals Unlimited (bottom right); Page 2: Anthony Nex/Uniphoto (top left) Craig D. Wood (top right), Robert Maust/Photo Agora (bottom left), David F. Clobes (bottom right); Page 4: Uniphoto; Page 6: Bill Beatty/Visuals Unlimited (left), Uniphoto (right); Page 8: Tom McCarthy/Unicorn Stock; Page 10: Palma Allen (all photos); Page 12: Inga Spence/Tom Stack & Assoc. (top left), John Sohlden/Visuals Unlimited (top right), Bill Stanton/International Stock (middle right), Ernest A. Janes/Bruce Coleman (bottom right), Uniphoto (bottom left); Page 14: Scott Campbell/International Stock; Page 16: Cathy Gyory

Graph it!

By Lisa Trumbauer

Consulting Editor: Gail Saunders-Smith, Ph.D.

Consultar cia Williams,

Co fman,

Math Learni Dalton School

Yellow Umbrella Books

an imprint of Capstone Press
Mankato, Minnesota

Graphs help us put things in order.
You can learn a lot by graphing
and looking at graphs.
There are many kinds of graphs.

A picture graph uses pictures
to show how many things there are.
We want to know how many teeth
we lost this year.
For every tooth we lost,
we draw a tooth in the column
above our names.

Lost Tooth Chart

| Greg | Kim | Pat | Lisa |

Look at the puppies!
How many puppies of each color
can you count?
How many can you count in all?

Let's graph it!
We will use a picture graph.

Puppy Colors

Brown		
Black		
White with Brown Spots		
White with Black Spots		

A pie graph looks like a pie
cut into pieces.
These children are eating fruit.
Let's graph how many apples
and how many peaches
the children are eating.

The pie graph, or circle, equals all the fruit they are eating.
Each piece, or area, of the graph equals one piece of fruit.
We color one area red
for one apple
and one area yellow
for one peach.

Favorite Fruits

We want to show how many girls
and boys there are.
The pie graph equals
the whole group of children.
Each area of the graph
equals one child.

How Many Boys and Girls

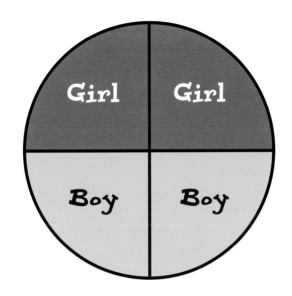

How many girls do we count?
We color 2 areas of the graph
red for 2 girls.

How many boys do we count?
We color 2 areas of the graph
yellow for 2 boys.

We count 2 girls and 2 boys.

A bar graph shows
how many in rows.
We want to show how many
blue, yellow, and green beads
have been taken out of the jar.
Count them.

Let's graph the number of colored beads from left to right in a row. Each box equals one ball.

We count the blue, yellow, and green boxes colored in each row. Which color has the least number of beads?

Which color has the most?

Colored Balls

	1	2	3	4	5	6	7	8
Blue	█	█	█					
Yellow	█	█	█	█	█	█	█	█
Green	█	█	█	█	█	█		

Let's go to the zoo.
We see 1 calf, 6 dogs,
3 goats, 2 cows, and 5 pigs.

Let's make a bar graph to show
how many of each animal
we see at the zoo!
How many more dogs
than cows?

Animals at the Zoo

	1	2	3	4	5	6
Calf						
Dog						
Goat						
Cow						
Pig						

These kids are wearing
their favorite colored shirts.
Let's graph how many shirts
there are of each color.